THE ROMNEY, HYTHE & DYMCHURCH RAILWAY

Contents

Front cover:
No 3 *Southern Maid* on Half Mile Curve with the 14.05 Hythe-Dungeness, 29 July 1984.
P. H. Groom

Back cover, top:
No 9 *Winston Churchill*. *P. H. Groom*

Back cover, bottom:
No 4 *The Bug*. *P. H. Groom*

First published 1985

ISBN 0 7110 1476 0

Published by Ian Allan Ltd. Shepperton, Surrey; and printed by Ian Allan Printing Ltd at their works at Coombelands in Runnymede, England.

Published by
IAN ALLAN LTD
Printed by Ian Allan Printing at their works at Coombelands in Runnymede, England

Acknowledgements

This book has aimed to describe the RH&DR in pictures, including an account of its history and origins, because that is an essential part of any description of an enterprise so unusual as 'The World's Smallest Public Railway'. But many parts of the story have been very difficult to illustrate, particularly in the sections dealing with the early years and before; and where photographs existed, often they have been impossible to use for technical reasons. Even so, the authors have tried to avoid the use of too many previously published pictures, and sometimes interest has been allowed to take priority over photographic quality. But above all, it is hoped that the book will succeed in giving a fair pictorial account of the railway with not too many blanks.

We should like to thank all those who have made photographs available to us; where the photographer is known, his name is given in each caption. Many pictures which we were regretfully unable to use were still valuable in settling various historical points, so thanks are due to many more people than whose names appear. In particular, we should wish to record thanks to Arthur Binfield and George Barlow, for their help in checking text and in making photographs available from their collections, A. L. S. Richardson, another of the original works team, and Terry Holder, involved with the railway from the visit of No 1 to Ravenglass in 1925 until his spell as Manager in 1946-48; Elenora and Ernest Steel, Henry Greenly's daughter and son-in-law; Derek and Sally Walsh for the loan of early postcards; the Bareham family for some valuable prewar photographs; Anthony Crowhurst, Bob Greenaway for their technical advice and assistance; Mrs J. Straton-Ferrier and Andrew Bowring (Howey's niece and nephew) for the loan of family photographs; Chris Leigh of Ian Allan for assistance in sorting through that company's picture library; Eric Youlden of Paxman Diesels Ltd (successors to Davey, Paxman Ltd); and members of the RH&DR Association and the railway's management and staff for their help and encouragement, particularly Michael Boatman (the Associa-tion's Chairman) and John Snell (the railway's Managing Director). In turn the two last-named have added to the text the note that the very considerable original work in collecting, selecting and describing the material for this book fell almost wholly on Paul Ross and Roger Lloyd-Smith, the Deputy-Chairman and recent Secretary respectively of the Association.

History of the Railway

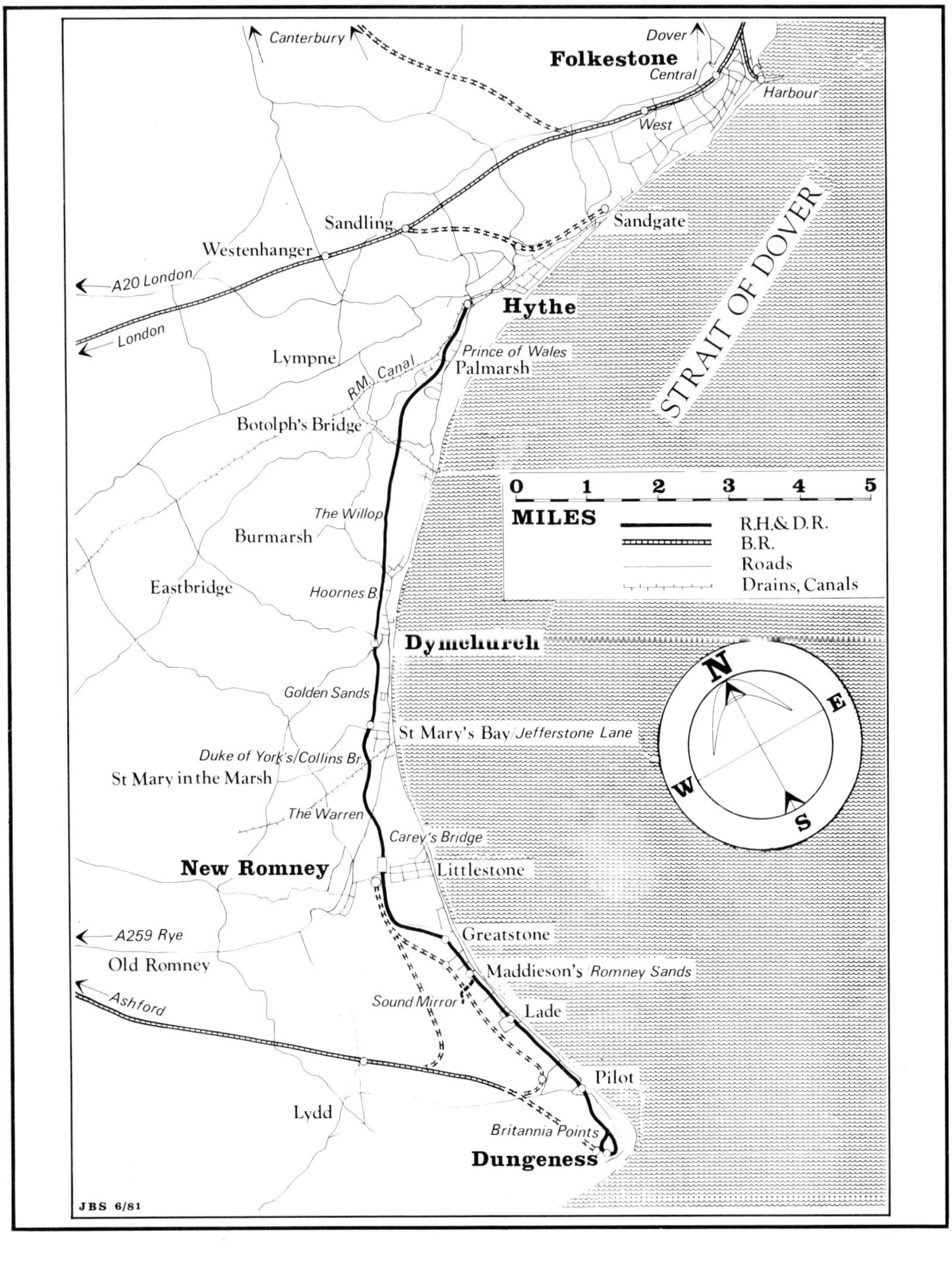

Map legend:

━━━	R.H.& D.R.	
┅┅┅	B.R.	
───	Roads	
┼┼┼	Drains, Canals	

0 1 2 3 4 5
MILES

Canterbury
Dover
Folkestone Central
Harbour
West
Sandgate
Sandling
Westenhanger
A20 London
London
Hythe
Lympne
Prince of Wales
R.M. Canal
Palmarsh
Botolph's Bridge
The Willop
Burmarsh
Eastbridge
Hoornes B
Dymchurch
Golden Sands
St Mary's Bay Jefferstone Lane
Duke of York's/Collins Br.
St Mary in the Marsh
The Warren
Carey's Bridge
New Romney
Littlestone
A259 Rye
Old Romney
Greatstone
Maddieson's Romney Sands
Ashford
Sound Mirror
Lade
Pilot
Lydd
Britannia Points
Dungeness

STRAIT OF DOVER

N E W S

JBS 6/81

The Romney, Hythe & Dymchurch Railway was the brainchild of two men, who met when they were each driving racing cars at Brooklands in 1921, and found they also shared an interest in miniature steam locomotives. Count Louis Zborowski, who had a Polish-American background, seems to have had the idea first of building somewhere a miniature mainline railway of a good length, complete with double track, stations and signalling, and plenty of live passengers. Captain J. E. P. Howey, who had by 1913 progressed from a boy's clockwork train set to having a 3ton 15in gauge Pacific locomotive running in his garden, was fired by the idea. In 1924 the two men jointly ordered a pair of much larger 15in gauge Pacifics to start their project and tried to buy the Ravenglass & Eskdale line in the Lake District, with a view to extending it. Unfortunately, later that year Zborowski was killed in a racing accident. Howey continued on his own, partly as a memorial to his friend, and in 1925 found the site for his railway at last, in taking up the abandoned proposal of the 1880s to extend the standard gauge Appledore to New Romney branch across Romney Marsh through Dymchurch to Hythe; 8¼ miles of level going fit for high speed trains.

The railway was built very quickly, and opened in July 1927 from New Romney to Hythe; Howey found nearly all the money out of his own pocket (over £140,000, the equivalent of about £4 million today). It was an immediate success with summer holidaymakers, so much so that Howey decided to extend it for another 5½ miles from New Romney to Dungeness, across country that was at that time almost all bare shingle beach. This extension was completed in

DIVE WITH DEAD PILOT

Lieutenant-Observer J. Howey, attached to the Royal Flying Corps, who is now a prisoner in Mainz after a thrilling dive in an aeroplane into the German lines. When 10,000ft. up his companion was killed by a fragment of shell, and the aeroplane im...

August 1928, though for a few months before that trains ran as far as The Pilot. Until 1940 trains ran daily throughout the year, carrying passengers (and a little freight), with the miniature steam locomotives running through

Below:
In 1911 J. E. P. Howey obtained his first miniature locomotive, this 9½in gauge version of a GNR Ivatt Atlantic, designed by Henry Greenly and built by the firm of Bassett-Lowke in Northampton. Here he stands behind his machine in 1912, at his home, Staughton Manor near Huntingdon, where Greenly was building for him a ¾-mile railway complete with a miniature Forth Bridge.

the summer and most of the winter traffic, much lighter, being operated by internal-combustion locomotives, among the first on any public railway in Britain. During the war the line was requisitioned by the Army and used for military traffic, being patrolled in 1940-41 by an armoured train, since of course the Romney beaches were the likeliest place for the threatened invasion. Much battered by the bombing and by heavy work, the railway was repaired and reopened for business in March 1946, one of the first holiday attractions to get back to normal. Dungeness was reached again in 1947.

From 1946 to 1955 the railway had its busiest years, before Londoners drove north or west along better roads in their new family cars for their holidays, or went instead on packages to the Costa Brava and other such places. Traffic has never since reached those levels, though it remains very substantial, nowadays including many who come out on a day trip from London or other centres. Since 1977 it has once again had some year-round trade, bringing 200 or so secondary schoolchildren to school in New Romney every day from homes in the Dymchurch area.

Howey died in 1963; running the railway had been his life's work and main interest since 1927. His widow sold the company the following year to S. H. Collins and J. E. Scatcherd, two retired bankers, who in turn sold it in 1968 to a group of Folkestone business men. Both groups made a start on rebuilding and renovation, which had become necessary after 40 years, but the financial implications were too adverse and the railway was threatened with closure in 1971. But instead it was acquired by a new group, led by W. H. McAlpine, in 1972.

Above:
In 1913 Howey converted the Staughton Manor line to 15in gauge and commissioned Bassett-Lowke and Greenly to produce a Pacific locomotive, only the second to run in Britain (after the GWR *Great Bear*). Named *John Anthony* after Howey's young son, the engine was in Howey's possession for only a short time, being sold in 1916 (while Howey was a prisoner of war) to the Ravenglass & Eskdale Railway, who renamed it *Colossus*. It is seen here at Beckfoot, about 1919.

Right:
Lieutenant-Observer J. Howey, attached to the Royal Flying Corps, early in 1915. He was taken prisoner later that year when his pilot was killed by a shell fragment while flying at 10,000ft, and the untrained Howey had to climb into the dead man's cockpit and fly the aircraft to a safe landing behind German lines.

Below:
Count Louis Zborowski and Howey met at Brooklands in 1921, where both drove racing cars, and during the next few years began to plan to build an ambitious 15in gauge main line railway in miniature. Here Zborowski sits at the wheel of one of his formidable 23-litre Mercedes-Maybach 'Chitty Bang Bangs'. *National Motor Museum*

Left:
Zborowski had a 15in gauge railway of his own at Bridge, near Canterbury, and just before he was killed racing at Monza in 1924 he took delivery of the last of the Bassett-Lowke-Greenly Atlantics to run on it. Subsequently sold to the Fairbourne Railway in Wales and named *Count Louis*, the locomotive ultimately visited the RH&DR and is shown here at Hythe in 1977.
J. B. Snell

Below:
In 1924 Zborowski and Howey jointly ordered a pair of greatly enlarged and improved 15in gauge Pacifics, designed by Henry Greenly and built by Davey Paxman of Colchester. Greenly sits in the cab of LZ1, newly completed; Zborowski did not live to see it finished in 1925. Howey later acquired it and named it *Green Goddess*.

Bottom:
In June 1925 *Green Goddess* ran trials on the Ravenglass & Eskdale Railway, and is seen pausing with a stone train near Irton Road. Howey sits at the throttle; Greenly in a straw boater in the first wagon. Both the original engines were at first fitted with Westinghouse brake, as well as vacuum; note the pump.

Above:
LZ1 on bench test in Davey, Paxman's works.

Below:
As concrete evidence of his plans, Howey put *Green Goddess* into Binns'
Garage, New Romney, during the Light Railway Order proceedings in 1926.
In the background he alights from his Hispano-Suiza.

Below left:
Later in 1925 Howey decided to go ahead on his own with the project of
building a miniature main line railway which he had discussed with
Zborowski, having at last found a suitable site, on Romney Marsh between
New Romney and Hythe. In November 1925 he posed on the site of New
Romney station for press photographers, with Greenly at the theodolite.
Construction was already under way, while lawyers and others struggled to
catch up with progress.

Above and left:
The first train on the RH&DR was a Royal Special, on 5 August 1926, when the track reached only from New Romney to the Duke of York's Camp at St Mary's Bay. With the Duke of York (later King George VI) driving, Howey also on the footplate, and Nigel Gresley, Chief Mechanical Engineer of the London & North Eastern Railway, sitting on the back of the tender, the train leaves New Romney on its return to the Camp; the engine is LZ2, by now named *Northern Chief*.

Below:
Even though steam shovels were available in 1926, the RH&DR was built by pick and shovel methods. The construction gang at the cutting at the Prince of Wales Bridge, West Hythe; the bridge itself was in the new material of reinforced concrete.
A. R. W. Crowhurst collection

Top:
The train shed under construction at Hythe; in the background, the foundations of the Light Railway Restaurant building, which Howey sold before the railway opened. Greenly's wife and daughter test the platform edging.

Above:
To assist with construction work, and subsequently for use as a shunting engine, a small 0-4-0 tender engine named *The Bug* was built by Krauss of Munich in 1926. During winter 1927 it worked on the Dungeness extension, here just south of New Romney. Some important visitor was evidently expected.

Right:
Original designer and builder of the RH&DR and a man of great achievements in the development and popularisation of model engineering; Henry Greenly at New Romney.
Elenora Greenly

Top:
Opened on 16 July 1927 between New Romney and Hythe, the railway attracted large crowds. During the first few weeks of running, *Southern Maid* pauses at Dymchurch with a train for New Romney.

Above:
The earliest coaches on the line were eight-seater four-wheelers, not one of Greenly's better ideas. They were rough-riding and unfitted for bad weather, though some had motor-car-type sidescreens; within 10 years they had all been withdrawn. *Southern Maid* at Burmarsh Road in 1927, returning tender-first to Hythe.
L&GRP courtesy David & Charles

Left:
During 1927 Greenly therefore designed, for winter use, certainly the best coaches ever to run on a 15in gauge railway; three compartment 12-seaters with steam heat and electric light. Eight were built by the Clayton Wagon Co and delivered in 1928. Two of Greenly's friends pose for his camera in one at New Romney.

Above:
The interior of a Clayton compartment; comfort equal to a contemporary main line third-class coach.

Above right:
A train arriving at Hythe, shortly after opening. *Lens of Sutton*

Above:
The original turntable at New Romney was simple but troublesome; Howey watches the gang freeing it to allow a locomotive off the shed.

Above:
Before being delivered to New Romney, No 7 *Typhoon* was sent to King's Cross Top Shed and photographed alongside Big Brother, Gresley's No 4472 *Flying Scotsman*. Now the last surviving example of Gresley's non-streamlined Pacifics, No 4472 belongs to the present Vice-Chairman of the RH&DR, The Hon W. H. McAlpine. *Bareham collection*

Below:
During construction, *Green Goddess* approaches the Warren Bridge with a trainload of workmen returning to New Romney. Note the miniature telegraph pole; the RH&DR had its own pole route until the 1950s.

Above:
The end of 1927 saw Howey with his ambition achieved. He now owned a fully operational passenger carrying railway providing a public service; and until he died in 1963, running it was his main interest in life. That there would be problems was no doubt obvious to him, but his confidence is apparent in this photograph of him on the footplate of one of the first two Pacifics in the yard at New Romney.

Below:
The RH&DR was not the only narrow gauge railway on Romney Marsh; from 1895 to 1939 there was also the 3ft gauge Rye & Camber. One of the two Bagnall 2-4-0Ts at Camber Sands. *L&GRP courtesy David & Charles*

Above right:
Closed stations: Botolph's Bridge Halt. 2½ miles from Hythe, this halt did little business and not long after this photograph was taken in the mid-1930s, was closed down summarily one evening by Howey, with a tin of petrol and a box of matches. The police were not amused.
G.A. Barlow collection

Right:
Closed stations: Greatstone Dunes. The lavish original layout at this point reflected the intention to terminate some trains here. Traffic expectations were disappointing, and nothing remains now except the left-hand shelter, incorporated into a fortification during the war.
L&GRP courtesy David & Charles

Below:
The famous works photograph showing five RH&DR locomotives under construction in the Davey, Paxman works at Colchester. Nos 1 and 2 had been completed earlier; Howey ordered No 3 (completed in the foreground), in March 1926, and No 4 *The Bug* shortly afterwards; then ordered another four locomotives from Paxmans during August 1926, Nos 5-8 inclusive. They differed from Nos 1-3, however; the design of 5 and 6 were modified at the County Council's request to cater for freight traffic, so they became 4-8-2s with smaller driving wheels, while Nos 7 and 8, although 4-6-2s outwardly identical with Nos 1-3, had three cylinders the same size as the earlier engines' two, and so a theoretical 50% increase in power (hardly achieved in practice).

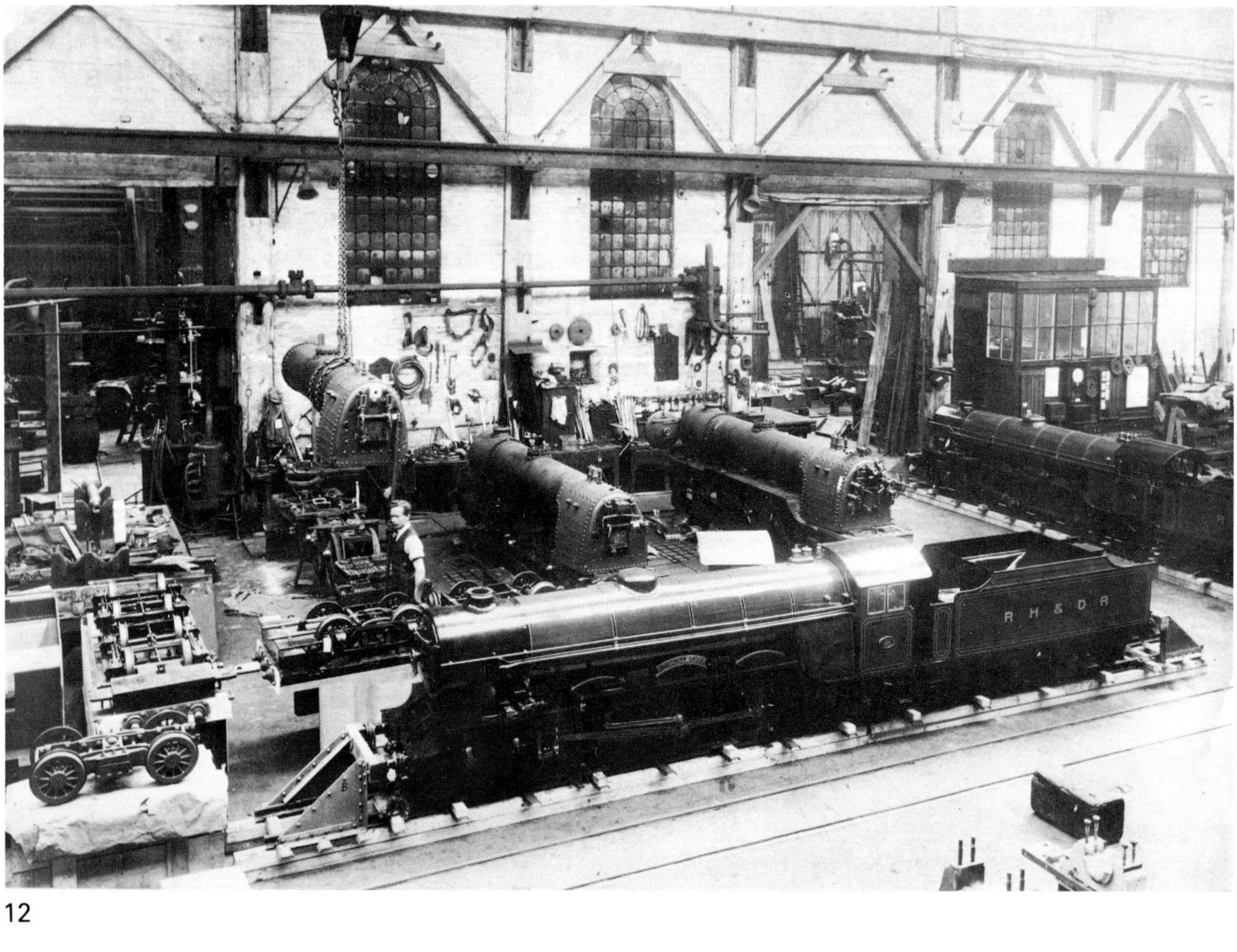

Above:
The Duke of York's special train waiting for him at the bridge later named after him, near St Mary's Bay. Greenly and Howey are on the footplate. Greenly had built a model Forth Bridge of 20ft span, for Howey's 9½in gauge garden railway in 1912; but despite its 56ft span this bridge, the longest on the RH&DR was a poor thing in comparison, not very impressive in design and flimsy in construction. It was condemned and replaced by a simpler structure in 1968. *Topical*

Below:
The original station at New Romney was not very conveniently laid out, especially after the Dungeness line opened. A school party crossing the main line to enter a train of four-wheelers about 1930. *Fox Photos*

Operating the Railway 1927~1945

Above:
The railway soon became a very popular attraction, for school parties as well as families on holiday. Here a rather rumbustious schools special, double-headed, leaves New Romney in the early 1930s, clients hanging out of the windows to be photographed. *Fox Photos*

Above:
Like many other railways in flat country, the RH&DR has always been plagued by level crossings, though now there is a programme to fit them all with automatic signals. One of the 4-6-2s crosses Burmarsh Road in front of a prudent motorist about 1938. *Fox Photos*

Left:
Daily services were operated from the beginning, right through the winter, and the RH&DR was one of the first railways in Britain to experiment with internal-combustion power to handle light traffic more economically than steam. Theakston of Crewe supplied the first ic locomotive in 1929, shown here; it was powered by a Model T Ford engine, and somewhat resembled a machine on the Ravenglass & Eskdale about the same time. With a maximum speed of about 15mph, it was not a success and withdrawn after a couple of years. *E. A. Beet*

Below:
Much more successful was the second ic locomotive, seen here leaving New Romney for Hythe in May 1936. Using the engine, gearbox and radiator from Howey's Silver Ghost Rolls-Royce of 1914, it was capable of speeds over 60mph. *H. C. Casserley*

Above:
The Rolls-Royce locomotive on a winter train at Hythe, about 1931.

Left:
No 8 *Hurricane* in the locomotive shed at New Romney, soon after the line was opened. Raising the rails on cast-iron stilts made access easier for repairs to springs and motion.
L&GRP courtesy David & Charles

Below left:
Six of these 6ton bottom-discharge hopper wagons were purchased from the Eskdale line in 1930, after they had been superseded there by construction of the standard gauge line to Murthwaite. The RH&DR used them mainly for adding ballast to its permanent way.
E. A. Beet

Top right:
Open and closed four-wheeled coaches, and some wagons, on the goods tranship siding at New Romney in 1928. The closed coach is one of several converted to luggage vans, with barred windows.
E. A. Beet

Centre right:
For some 20 years before and after the war, Howey's friend Colonel Tyrrell had a half-mile-long 7½in gauge line running beside the RH&DR Tyrrell's 0-4-4T *Atalanta* being passed by No 10, then named *Black Prince* in 1938.
R. M. Tyrrell

Bottom right:
Dymchurch station about 1938, showing the long-vanished signalbox and overall roof, as well as the narrow platforms. This station was originally intended to accommodate short-working trains to and from New Romney only, in the bay platform to the right; but this facility was never completed since it was found to be unnecessary. For many years some trains did reverse at Dymchurch, but they worked to and from Hythe, and always used the main line platforms. *L&GRP courtesy David & Charles*

16

Above:
During 1940 an armoured train was built for the RH&DR, consisting of 4-8-2 No 5 *Hercules* fitted with some rather scanty armour cladding and two of the ex-Eskdale ballast hoppers, more heavily armoured in the central well section and fitted each with a pair of Lewis guns and a Boyes anti-tank rifle. Until the danger of invasion receded, this train was kept with steam up at all times, in a siding near Dymchurch. It is seen here at Dymchurch station.
Imperial War Museum

Below left:
Another view of *Hercules*, as fitted to work the armoured train.
Imperial War Museum

Below right:
The fastest thing on rails was this motor scooter, powered by a 6hp JAP motorbike engine, which Howey had built in 1929, and on which he once reached Hythe from New Romney in eight minutes. He evidently kept it off the rails, lest anybody else should get similar ideas. Sitting on it in front of the machine shop at New Romney is Arthur Binfield, the workshop apprentice during the early years. *A. A. Binfield*

The Locomotives and the Rolling Stock

The Locomotives

By 1924, Henry Greenly had become well known as a designer of miniature railways and locomotives, and both as a model engineer and a writer in and editor of journals catering for the new hobby of model engineering. He had had more experience than anyone else in Britain of designing 15in gauge locomotives intended to do commercial work on short lines in parks, zoos, or seaside resorts, and on the Ravenglass & Eskdale Railway, which on the bed of an abandoned 3ft gauge line had in 1916 begun to run as the first 15in gauge railway in the world offering a regular public transport service. When in that year Howey and Zborowski commissioned him to design a pair of 15in gauge locomotives modelled on arguably the fastest and most powerful British mainline express passenger locomotives of the day, the Gresley Pacifics of the London & North Eastern Railway, Greenly's experience had taught him the most important lesson, that scale models were no good for commercial service; they turned out too weak and flimsy. On track one quarter of standard gauge, you needed a locomotive that was, in its proportions, one third of full size, and in its mechanical details – bearing sizes and so on – stronger still.

When it was completed in 1925, Howey took the first locomotive, which he named *Green Goddess*, to Ravenglass for some test runs; then, as his project on Romney Marsh matured, he took both machines to New Romney and ordered five more. The second engine he named *Northern Chief* before the Duke of York (later King George VI) visited the still-building line that year; the third, almost identical, was at first called *Southern Chief* but Howey soon had second thoughts and changed it to *Southern Maid*. The fourth was a small four-wheeled shunting engine, mainly used in construction of the Dungeness line, a 15in gauge variant of their smallest line of standard contractors' 2ft gauge tank engines built by Krauss of Munich, and christened *The Bug*. Nos 5 and 6, like Nos 1 to 3, were built by Davey Paxman of Colchester, but these were modified to make them more suitable for

Above:
No 1 *Green Goddess* as running during the 1970s, on the turntable at Hythe. Although now reboilered, like all the other original RH&DR locomotives, and superheated, she has changed relatively little from her 1925 condition, except for receiving a new high-capacity tender in the late 1940s. She received her third tender in 1983.
P. H. Groom

the freight traffic which the Kent County Council had asked the railway to cater for, ballast from the quarry at West Hythe. Otherwise similar to Nos 1-3, they had eight small driving wheels instead of six large ones. No 5 was called *Hercules* and No 6 *Samson*. Nos 7 and 8 differed again; otherwise the same as 1-3, they were given a third cylinder, like the Gresley engines they resembled, in the hope that they would prove more powerful, they were named *Typhoon* and *Hurricane*. The first winter of operation showed that the drivers could do with better protection from the weather, and Greenly had the idea of producing miniature versions of some North American locomotives, in particular a Canadian Pacific type. These were usually built higher and wider than British types, with

bigger and better cabs. It was intended to build Nos 9 and 10 at New Romney, with some parts supplied by Davey Paxman, but plans changed and they were ultimately completed in 1931 by the Yorkshire Engine Co in Sheffield.

There were and are also a number of small petrol or diesel locomotives, used for inspection and maintenance work along the line. To deal with light winter passenger trains Howey had built in 1929 and 1930 two larger petrol locomotives, the second of which used parts of an old Rolls-Royce he had and was a success, lasting until 1962. In 1976 the RH&DR purchased secondhand another Pacific, which had been built by Krupp for the Düsseldorf exhibition of 1937 (two more identical locomotives had earlier been acquired by Alan Bloom, of Bressingham Hall in Norfolk). In 1983 the railway had built its third non-steam locomotive, by TMA Engineering in Birmingham; but unlike its two predecessors, which were designed for light winter trains, No 12 is intended for heavy trains at all times of the year, and so is rather more powerful than any of the steam

Left:
No 2 *Northern Chief* retained her original small tender until she was overhauled in 1982 and took over the high-capacity tender from *Green Goddess*, passing her original tender on to *Hercules*. Like her co-senior *Green Goddess* she is not greatly changed from her 1925 condition, apart from receiving smoke deflectors and new straight nameplates in the 1950s. Captain Howey made this change to several RH&DR Pacifics to make them resemble the postwar LNER Peppercorn locomotives. *P. H. Groom*

Below:
No 3 *Southern Maid* outside New Romney shed at night. She still retains her postwar high-capacity tender, but lost the smoke deflectors which Howey fitted when overhauled in 1970. *J. R. Carter*

Right:
Resurrected from the Belfast scrapyard and rebuilt in 1976, No 4 *The Bug* now belongs to W. H. McAlpine, but is normally based at New Romney and used on special occasions, as here, crossing New Cut Bridge. *P. H. Groom*

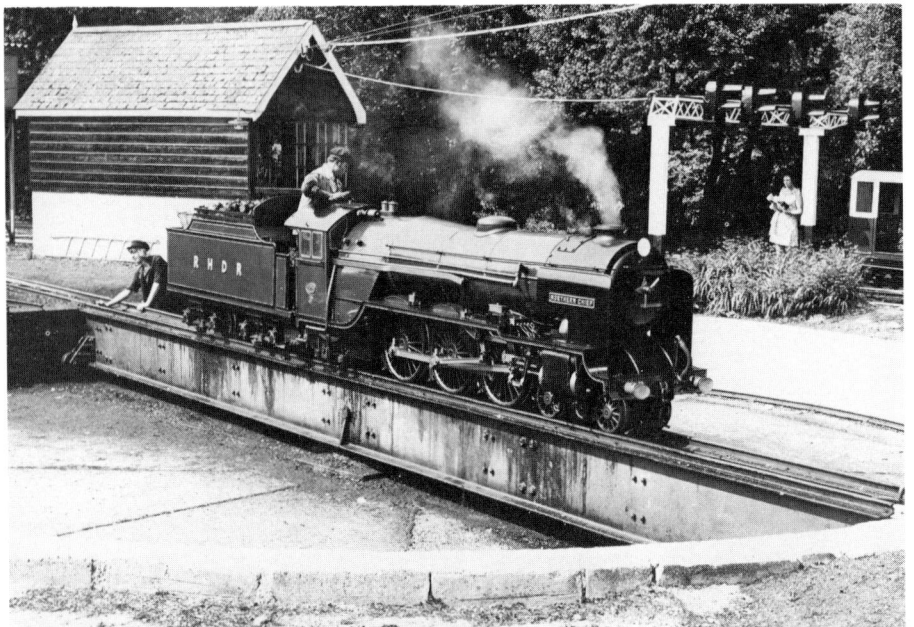

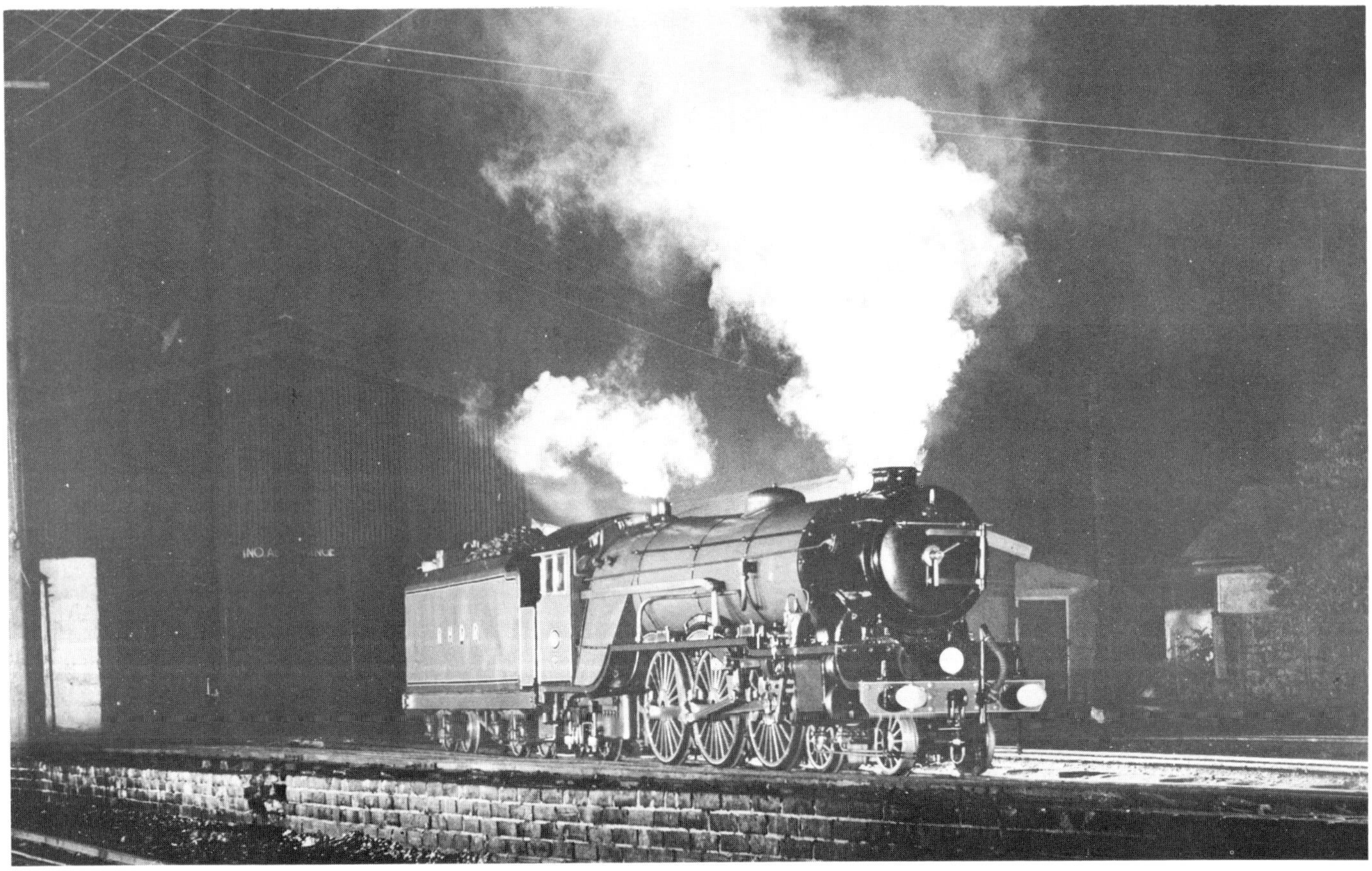

locomotives. Unlike them again, it was designed to do a particular job rather than to resemble some mainline type of machine, but all the same it does somewhat resemble a typical modern American diesel.

Rolling Stock

For the opening of the railway, Greenly provided over 100 four-wheeled eight-seater coaches of rather spartan character, modelled on the standard small coaches Mr Bassett-Lowke supplied to rich Edwardians for their garden railways, complete with canvas roof and frilly fringe. Adequate for that purpose, they were a disaster at Romney speeds and lengths of run, rough and uncomfortable, even though Greenly had taken great care to make them low enough not to be blown over by high winds. Howey quickly had built eight very fine 12-seater bogie coaches, with steam heat and electric light, and then a further 54 more eight-seater bogie coaches, fully enclosed and with extremely comfortable seating; by 1939 almost none of the original coaches were left.

No prewar coaches still remain in service, and more than half the present fleet of 60 or so has been renewed since 1970. Present plans are to standardise on three main types of coach: 20-seater saloons, with longer bodies; 20-seater opens, with roofs but open sides, for summer use; and at least one guard's and luggage van per train. But many older and smaller vehicles will remain in service for some years yet, particularly some 16-seaters dating from the 1960s. There are also some special vehicles, including the Directors' Saloon, and the famous Bar Car, with drinks and light refreshments served on board by an attendant, which is incidentally 32ft long and, in relation to track gauge, certainly the longest single-unit railway vehicle in the world.

Freight rolling stock nowadays consists of vehicles used for maintenance purposes and carrying supplies up and down the line, mainly four-wheeled and bogie flat trucks, but including some ballast tippers and two of the original low-sided trucks. There are also specialised items, like the rail-carrying set and the rail-mounted concrete mixer, air compressor, and generator sets.

Above:
4-8-2 No 5 *Hercules*, although she worked the first passenger train from Hythe in 1927, saw little service before the war. Overhauled by the Southern Railway at Ashford in 1946, she received a new high-capacity tender, which by mistake was designed to suit one of the CPR engines, and was badly oversize for the others. For a time (as here in 1947) the cab roof was raised to try to correct matters. Later the tender was reduced in height, but it has now been scrapped and *Hercules* now has an original small tender.
K. A. C. R. Nunn

Below:
Hercules on Half Mile Curve, south of New Romney, after a high wind had caught a four-wheeled guards' van in the train, of a now-extinct type called Jumping Jacks by the staff, and caused a chain reaction of unfortunate circumstances. *G. A. Barlow*

Right:
No 6 *Samson* receiving a critical examination at New Romney. *P. H. Groom*

Below:
No 7 *Typhoon* outside Hythe shed in 1976. In company with No 8, this engine was built with three cylinders, but the extra power was not necessary while the extra complexity was too great, so both engines were converted to two-cylinder during the 1930s. *P. H. Groom*

Bottom:
No 8 *Hurricane* was always Captain Howey's personal locomotive, and still has some special touches like stainless steel handrails. It received the first high-capacity tender, in 1934, to enable Howey to run non-stop from Hythe to Dungeness without worrying about water supply.
P. H. Groom

Left:
The idea of building two more locomotives to resemble a Canadian Pacific Railway class originated with the need for a larger cab to give the driver better protection against winter weather. However, the Vanderbilt tenders they had originally were an American touch; they were replaced with more conventional tenders in 1962. No 9, originally named *Doctor Syn* but now *Winston Churchill* at Hythe shortly after delivery in 1931. *K. A. C. R. Nunn*

Below:
No 10, *Doctor Syn* double-heading No 9 *Winston Churchill* approaching Dungeness on a Hythe to Hythe nonstop special in 1969. *T. R. Miller*

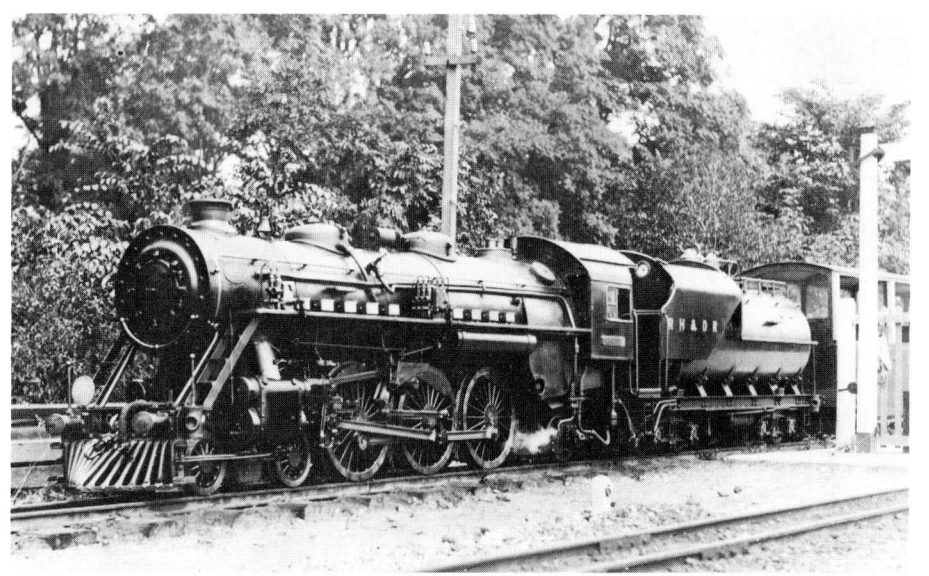

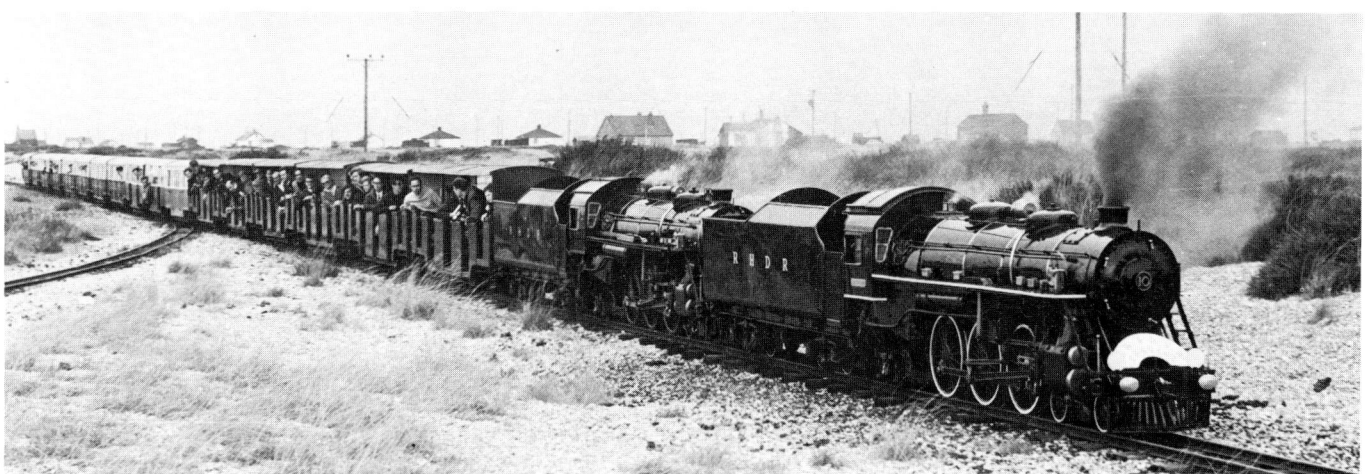

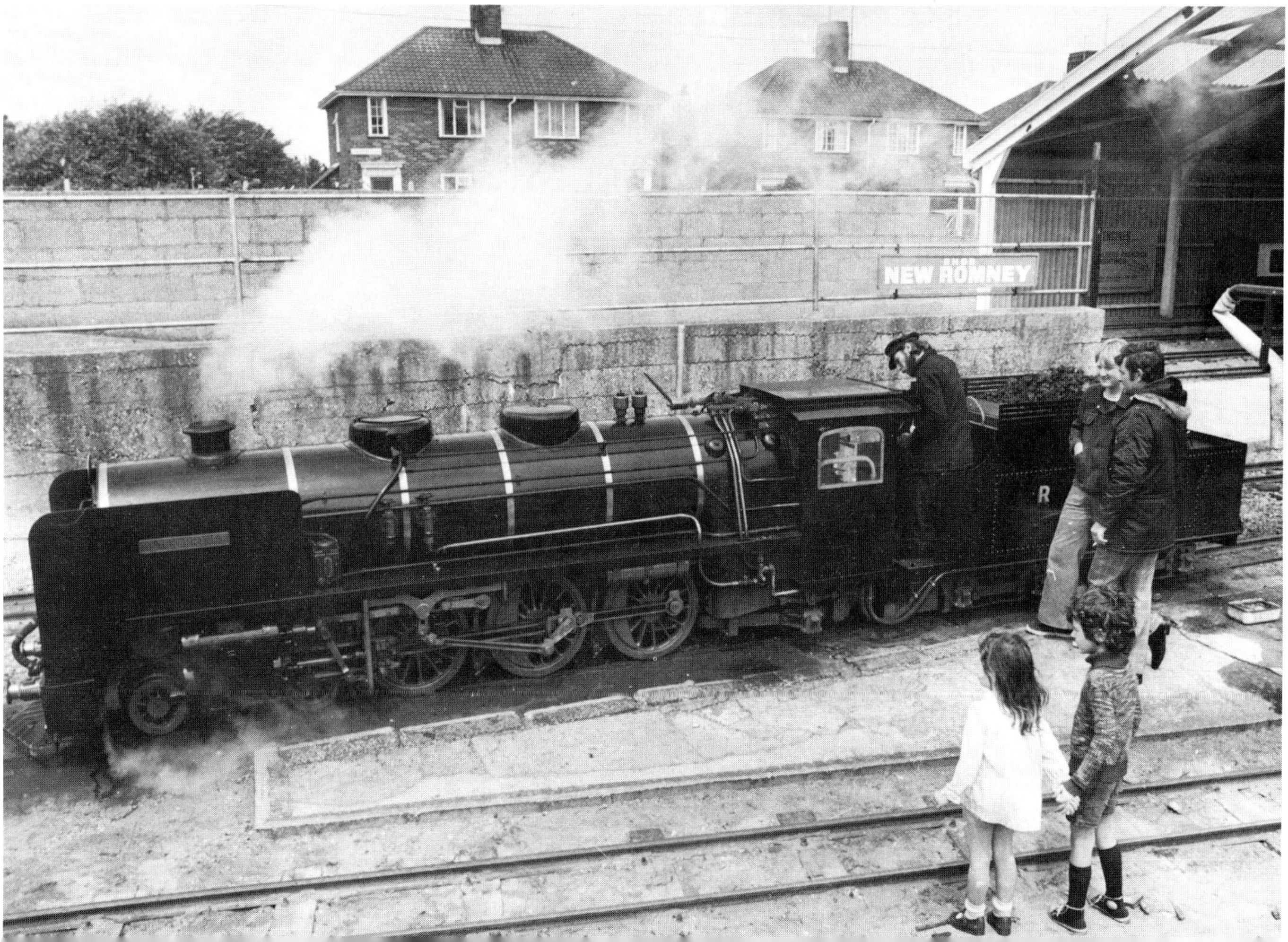

Bottom:
No 11 *Black Prince* was built by Krupp of Essen for the Dusseldorf exhibition of 1937 and acquired by the RH&DR in 1976, as an example of one of the very few other heavy-duty 15-in gauge steam locomotives ever built. The original name, *Fleissig Lieschen* or *Busy Lizzie*, was felt rather too lightweight for such a respectable machine. *Keystone*

Above right:
The Bug during its latter period in Belfast; low tide in the scrapyard.

Right and below:
Locomotives being prepared for the day's work at New Romney; *(right)* left to right, Nos 4, 6, 10 and 8; *(below)* Nos 10 and 7 being prepared for the day's work at New Romney. *P. H. Groom*

Above left:
Big fleas have little fleas; *The Bug* meets a one-third size, 5in gauge version of itself at New Romney. *J. C. Beckett*

Left:
Conventional steam locomotives use a lot of lubricating oil; driver Walsh gives *Hercules* a further dose on the slidebars. *D. Smalley*

Below:
In its last years, before it was scrapped in 1961, the Rolls-Royce saw little service, and in fact was no longer a Rolls-Royce, having been rebuilt with a Fordson engine and the radiator modified to suit. Seen here in the old carriage shed at New Romney in 1953. *A. G. Wells*

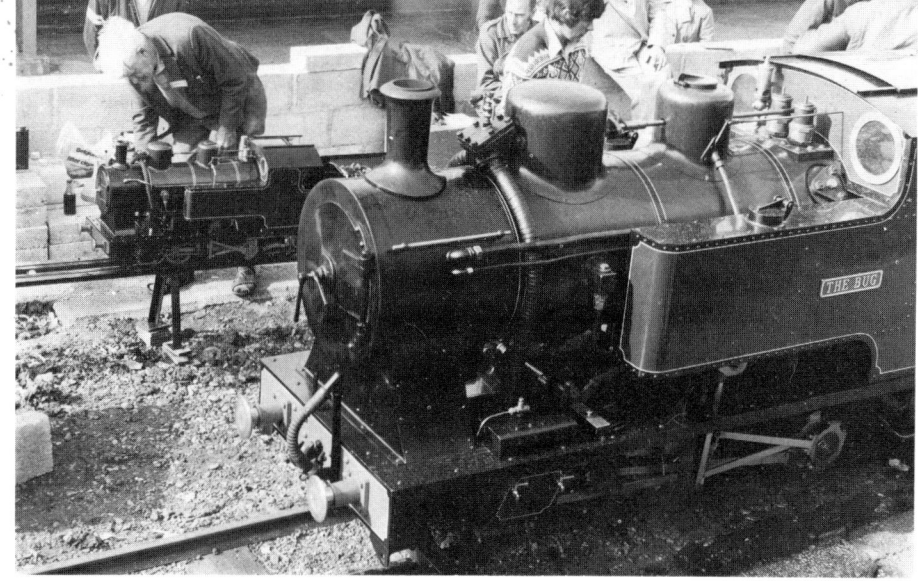

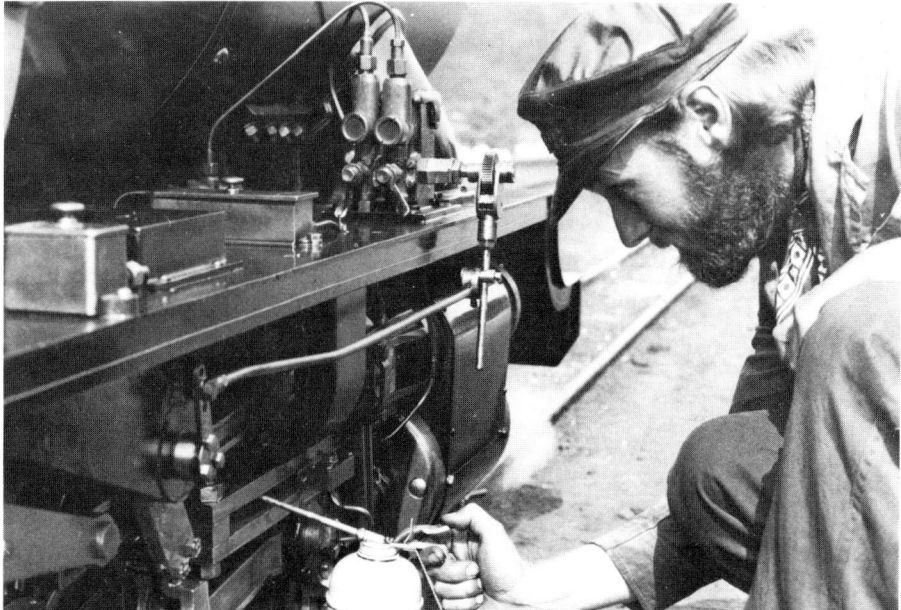

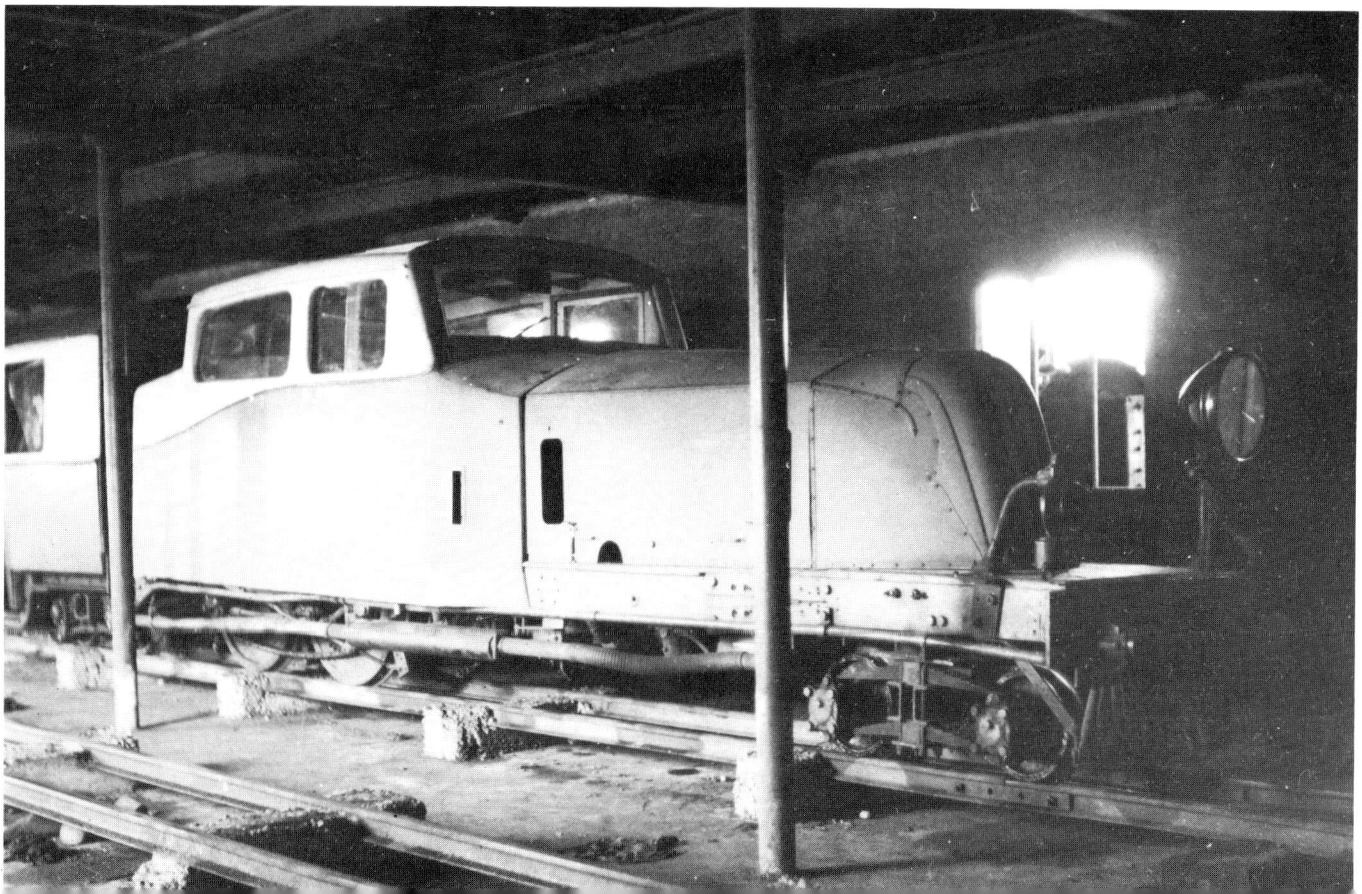

Above:
Winston Churchill on the turntable at Hythe in 1980. *P. H. Groom*

Left:
For some years in the 1970s, **Winston Churchill** was converted to burn oil, and fuelled up from a bowser at New Romney. *A. R. W. Crowhurst*

Below:
The original four-wheeled coaches which served the RH&DR at its opening were not successful, though their riding was somewhat improved by making some of them into articulated sets. Only one quad-set of articulated stock survived the war, having been used to carry steel pipe for the PLUTO projects; some cheap open bodies were put onto it in 1947 and it survived until 1960. *A. G. Wells*

Above:
Two of the 1934 batch of 16ft bogie coaches, destroyed during the war, were rebuilt as observation cars, named *Pluto* and *Martello*, during 1947. They seated ten people, and also like the bar car of 1977, were extra wide (4ft) to allow more space. Rather like a double-ended Gresley beavertail observation car, *Pluto* is seen here at Hythe in March 1947, about the time when Laurel and Hardy travelled in it. *A. G. Wells*

Left:
The five ex-Ravenglass & Eskdale 6ton ballast wagons which survived the war were rebuilt as passenger coaches in 1947, two of them as 18-seat observation cars like this example, in Pullman chocolate-and-cream livery and with Pullman crests. Passengers sat with their backs to the windows, and one central door on each side meant that entry and exit was a bit slow. Unfortunately all five bodies were too lightly built and had to be replaced after only a few years. *J. C. Flemons*

Below:
In 1950, following the death of his old school friend the Duke of Sutherland, Howey purchased the Duke's private engine, this little 0-4-4T *Dunrobin* and his private saloon, and kept them both at New Romney; occasionally they were exercised up and down the RH&DR standard gauge siding, otherwise used for delivering coal, though originally intended for general freight. In 1965 both were sold to an operator in British Columbia, where they still run. *G. A. Barlow*

Repairs and Improvements

Below left:
Heat causes rails to expand – and when it is combined with double track, the rails tend to move in the direction of traffic and so in effect expand at one end and contract at the other. Finally something gives way, as on this occasion at Star Dyke in the 1960s. Trains continued to run, rather gingerly.
RH&DR

Right:
The lowest point on the line, and some feet below mean sea level, is in the tunnel at New Romney, where sometimes the water table rises above the surface. No 5 approaches the resultant underground ford in 1981.
P. H. Groom

Below:
Captain Howey always disliked getting into the catering business; he sold off the station restaurant at Hythe before the railway opened, and for years passengers wanting refreshment were directed elsewhere. Terence Holder, manager of the railway from 1946, finally managed to get agreement to setting up this open air kiosk, using an old van body as stall building, at New Romney in 1947.

Below right:
The original station at Hythe could hardly have been more basic; apart from the roof over half the platform length, there was simply one small office hut, and passengers waiting to buy tickets often had to queue in the rain.

Bottom:
An early priority for the railway's new owners in 1972 was a better station at Hythe, and this temporary wooden building put up the following year contained a good concourse area and shop. At the same time some permanent new lavatories were built, replacing the unspeakable originals.
Keystone Press

Right:
The original tiny roof over the centre of the platforms at Dymchurch, looking as if it had escaped from a child's train set, which made the platforms inconveniently narrow, was demolished by volunteer working parties organised by the RH&DR Association during 1977; the job was not easy since blastproof walls, reinforced with many old tram rails, put up during the war, had to be removed. *R. Lloyd Smith*

Below:
The original small station office building at Dymchurch has been enlarged to include a shop and teabar, and surrounded with a verandah. *P. Ross*

Left:
The railway is laid on some 64,000 timber sleepers, and renewing these is a large part of the maintenance effort every winter. Retimbering the crossover at New Romney.

Top:
Between 1½ and 2 miles of track are relaid every winter, usually reusing most of the old rails, but nearly four miles of replacement rail have been laid in since 1970. Spiking down new rail near Jefferstone Lane in 1981.

Above:
Open, ungated and unsignalled, level crossings became an increasing problem after the 1940s, with increased road traffic, and after a series of accidents, with fatalities in 1946 and 1973, the RH&DR obtained the agreement of the local authorities to contribute to the cost of installing modern automatic signals at all the crossings between Hythe and New Romney. A programme of extending these to cover the crossings on the Dungeness line has now been commenced. *The Bug* on a special for Hythe crossing Burmarsh Road, Dymchurch.

Left:
Demolition of the Duke of York's Bridge under way in 1968. *Kent Messenger*

Right:
If hot days sometimes cause buckles, cold nights can naturally create the opposite problem; the cure is the same, basically a higher standard of maintenance. When the bolt breaks at a time like this, the stressed rails will suddenly jump apart by anything up to 2ft.   *A. R. W. Crowhurst*

Below:
RH&DR locomotives are capable of as much as 100,000 miles between major overhauls, but ultimately the time comes for a General Repair. *Hurricane* dismantled for this purpose in 1973.   *G. A. Barlow*

Bottom:
Major boiler repairs are generally given to a contractor; *Hercules's* boiler awaits completion of the engine's machinery at New Romney in 1979.   *P. H. Groom*

The Railway Today

The RH&DR is still owned and operated by the company which Howey founded to build and run it in 1926, and which was incorporated that year by a Light Railway Order under the Light Railways Act 1896. It is the ownership of the railway company which has changed several times; since 1972 practically all its shares have been held by a holding company, now called Romney Hythe & Dymchurch Railway PLC. This company in turn has over 600 shareholders, and these individuals and groups are the ultimate owners of the line. For practical reasons, a substantial minimum size of investment is necessary for a shareholding, and so the railway is also supported, both financially and with voluntary effort, by the Romney, Hythe & Dymchurch Railway Association, membership in which is open to all on payment of an annual subscription. The RH&DRA also publishes a quarterly magazine giving news about the railway, and its members get reduced rate travel on the line.

The railway company employs some 25 full-time staff the whole year round; these form the nucleus of the operating force in summer and concentrate on maintenance work during the winter. During the season as many more temporary staff are taken on to assist, including students and pensioners, so at the peak there are 60 or more on the payroll. Meeting this cost is a considerable burden, and when the very heavy additional expense of carrying out the long programme of renewals and improvements commenced in 1972 and not yet completed is taken into account, the railway has some difficulty in balancing its books. In fact the slow progress on improvement is a reflection of shortage of funds, and nothing more. If it was still visited by as many people as travelled on it 30 years ago, things would be different; but all the holiday attractions in southeast have suffered a decline over this period – Folkestone now has fewer than half the number of hotel beds it had 20 years ago – and the fact that the RH&DR is world famous has done little to help it avoid the same decline.

In 1969 and 1980 the question of moving the whole enterprise to another site, where more traffic potential existed, was considered – the first time in private, the second in public.

After all, BR line closures have left many suitable sites available! However, the local authorities in Kent are trying to arrest and reverse the decline of their tourist and holiday businesses, and in 1980 it was felt right to involve them in the question. Ultimately both the Kent County and Shepway District Councils gave some help to the railway, the SDC substantially by funding the purchase of the new diesel locomotive. With this heartening support, it remains RH&DR policy to do all it can to improve the railway on its present site.

Any additional support will however be much welcomed! In the first instance, anyone considering helping the railway, physically, financially, or only morally (with a small annual sub!) can obtain a leaflet giving particulars about the RH&DR Association from any station office or shop, or by writing to the Secretary, RH&DRA.

Below:
Northern Chief with a train of new aluminium coaches approaching the Warren. *P. H. Groom*

Above:
Samson approaching the Warren with a set of 'teak' 20-seater coaches, built in the early 1970s. The attractive natural varnished wood finish of this stock unfortunately had to be discontinued when the price of timber of good quality rose too high, and aluminium had to be used instead. *P. H. Groom*

Right:
Black Prince leaving Dungeness. *P. H. Groom*

Below:
Winston Churchill coming through the woods on the approach to New Romney, with a train from Dungeness. *P. H. Groom*

Above left:
Black Prince **leaving Dungeness with a train of rather variegated stock. While more than half the coaches on the railway have been built to standard designs since 1972, a number of non-standard 'one-offs' from earlier years survive as well as older stock not yet withdrawn, so not all trains present a very uniform appearance.** *P. H. Groom*

Left:
Diesel No 12, delivered in 1983, can be used in either direction if required, but is not seen so often on a train with its long hood leading. *P. H. Groom*

Below:
No 12 on a northbound train leaving New Romney.
P. H. Groom

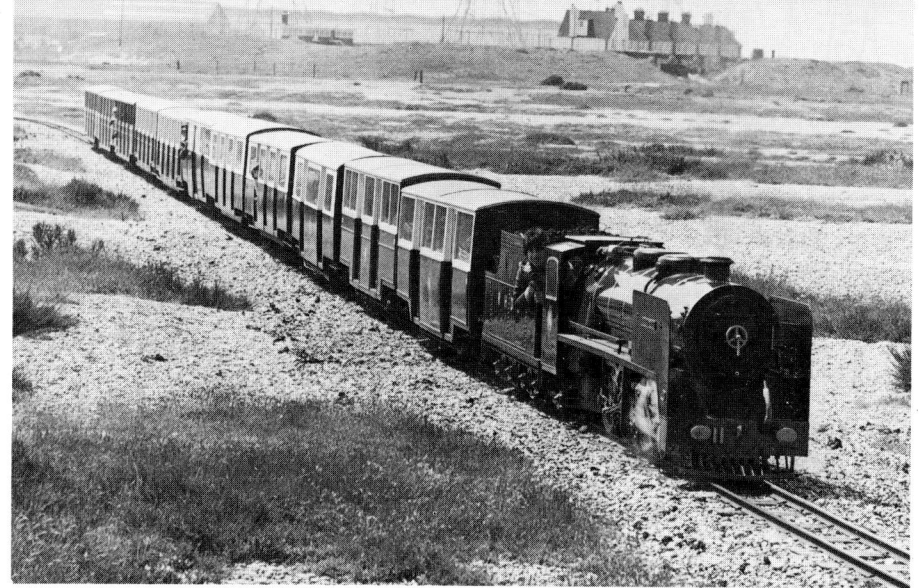

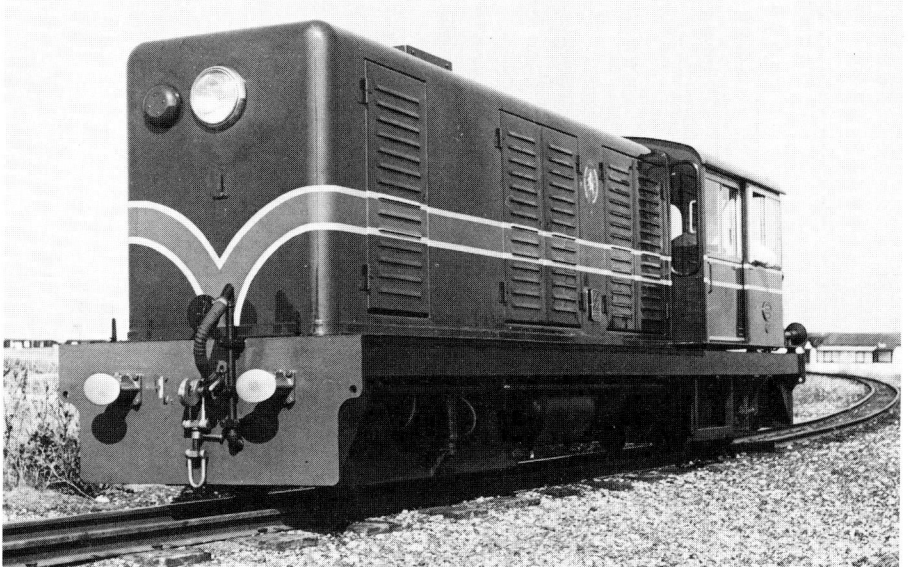

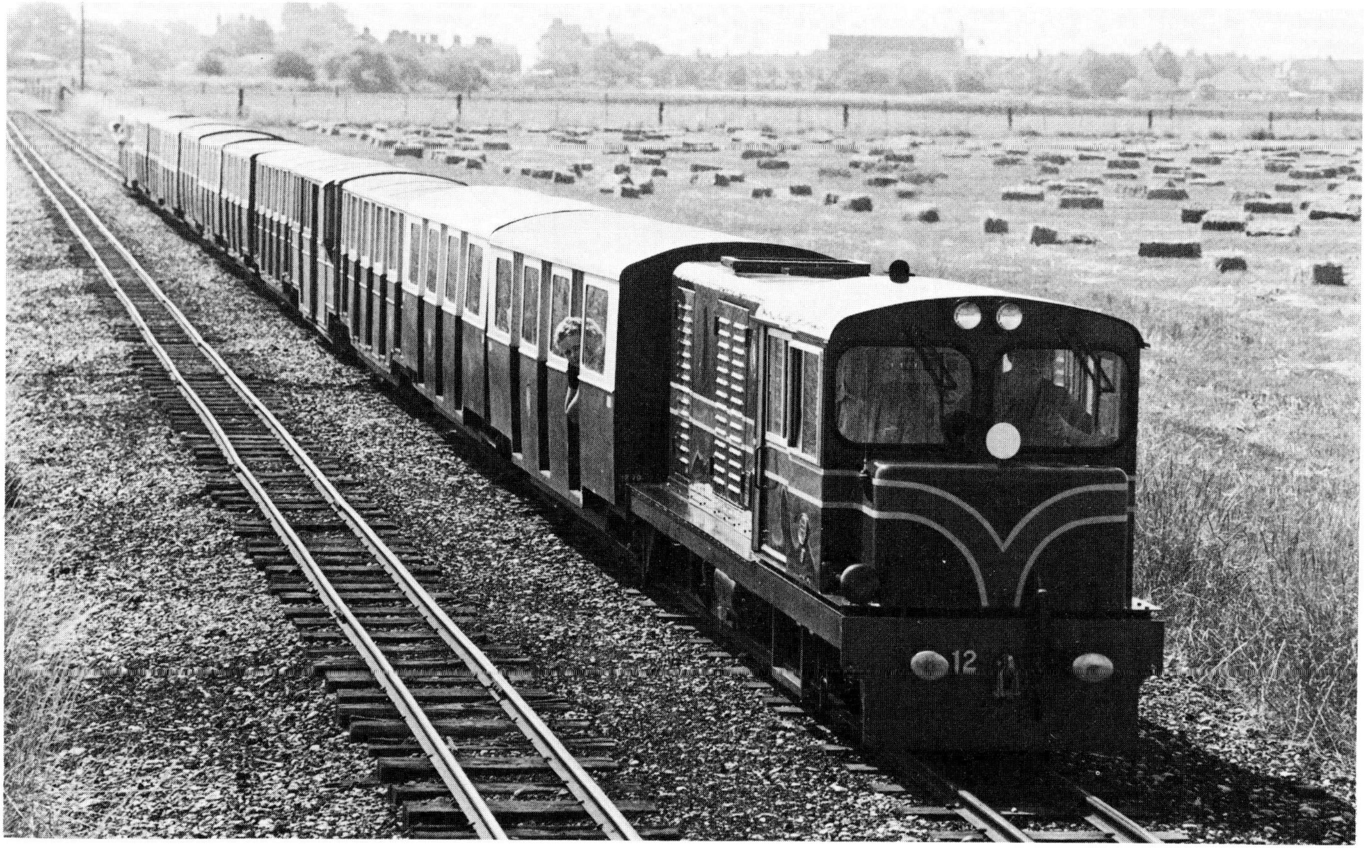

Right:
Doctor Syn on a southbound train near The Warren. *P. H. Groom*

Below:
Black Prince leaving Dungeness with a special. While most trains leave Dungeness in the opposite direction to proceed round the reversing loop, sometimes it is necessary for various reasons to keep the coaches the same way round without reversal, and in those cases the locomotive goes round the loop on its own and draws the train out the same way as it came in.
P. H. Groom

Bottom:
Southern Maid leaving New Romney for Dungeness. The first three coaches are 'opens', with no doors or windows, very popular in fine weather.
P. H. Groom

Right:
Looking towards the tunnel under Littlestone Road, New Romney.
P. H. Groom

Below:
Young revellers in the bar car salute the camera as their train leaves Dungeness. *P. H. Groom*

Bottom:
***Southern Maid* between The Pilot and Dungeness. The land hereabouts is mostly bare shingle, with low scrub and patches of grass in places; many of the houses are based on old standard gauge railway coach bodies.**
P. H. Groom

Left:
Northern Chief at New Romney, ex-works in 1982.
P. H. Groom

Below:
Winston Churchill approaching Britannia Points, at the north end of the Dungeness reversing loop, with a train from Hythe. *P. H. Groom*

Bottom:
The Bug on a special train from Hythe in August 1983, passing another train hauled by *Doctor Syn* at the Warren. Passengers leaning out – like the one in the first coach – are not encouraged to do so! *P. H. Groom*

Right:
Hercules at speed near Greatstone. *P. H. Groom*

Far right:
Winston Churchill receiving attention at New Romney shed. *P. H. Groom*

Bottom right:
No 12 passing the caravan camp at the Prince of Wales, West Hythe. Captain Howey originally contemplated building a station here, and acquired sufficient land to do so, visible on the right.
RH&DR

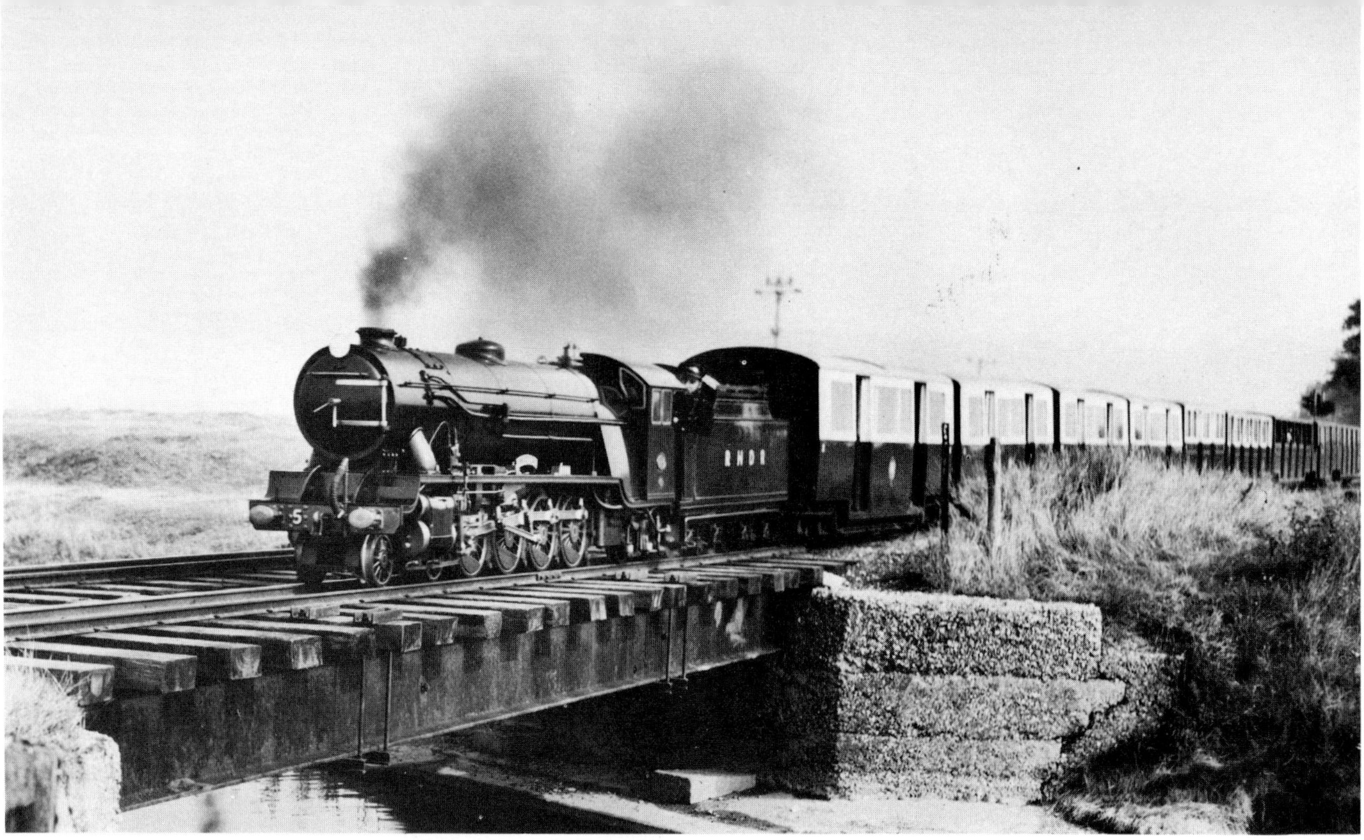

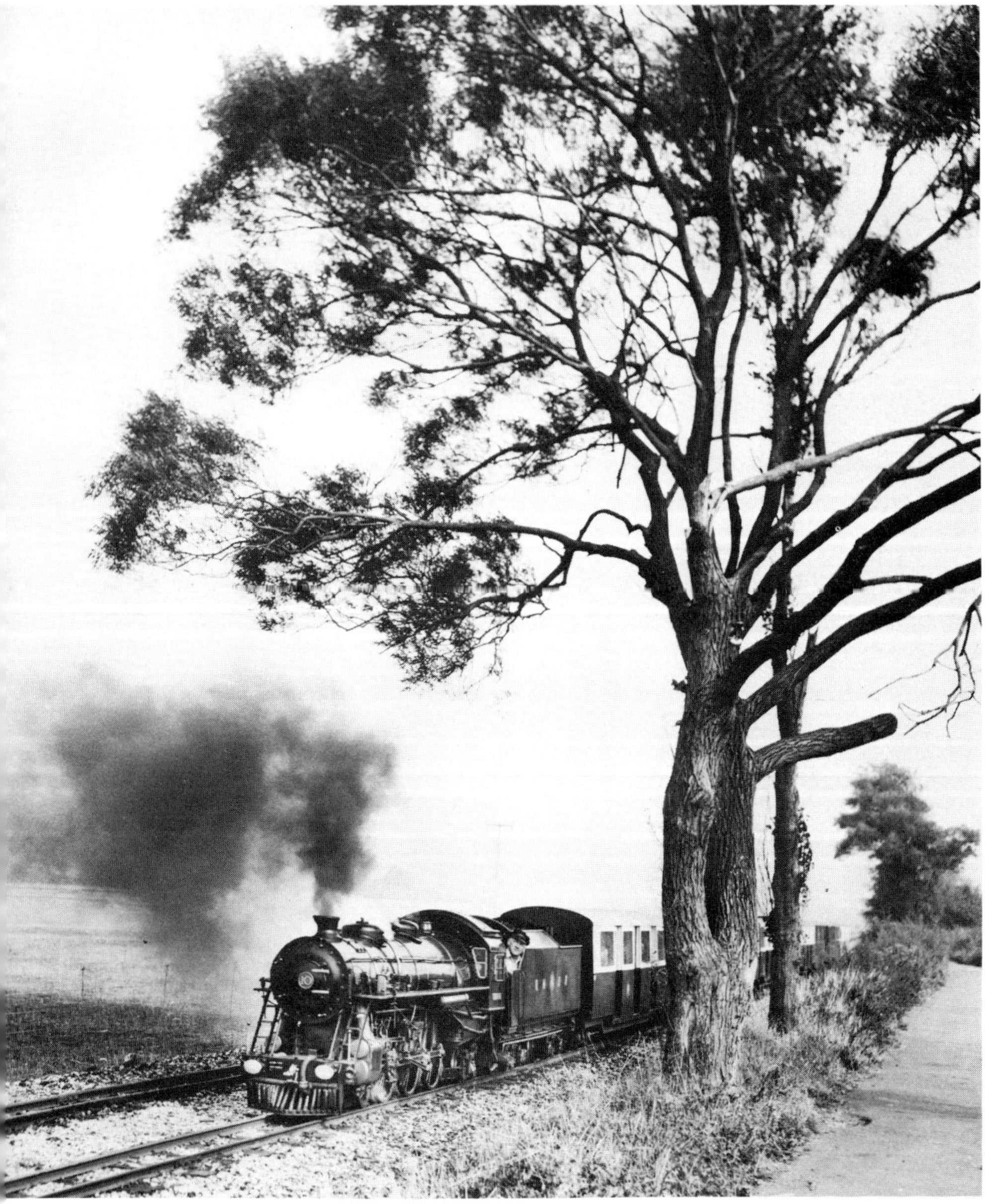

Above:
Hercules **on the bridge over the New Cut at Botolph's Bridge Road. This is one of the two underline bridges surviving from the opening of the railway; all the others were rebuilt during the 1960s and 1970s.** *Ron Ziel*

Left:
Doctor Syn **approaching Botolphs Bridge crossing, passing one of the few trees in the open marshland.** *Ron Ziel*

Above right:
For some 18 months in 1981-83, while its own diesel locomotive was being designed and built, the RH&DR borrowed the Ravenglass & Eskdale's 4-6-4 diesel-hydraulic locomotive, *Shelagh of Eskdale*, mainly to work the school train but also to take a share in ordinary traffic. While not an ideal machine for Romney conditions, she proved well able to do the work. She is seen here leaving Dungeness. *P. H. Groom*

Right:
The school train, carrying over 200 children to and from school in New Romney every day from the Dymchurch area, started to run in 1977 and was steam-hauled regularly until 1981. During a blizzard in early 1981, *Winston Churchill* is ready to leave New Romney with the afternoon train, piloted by the ex-Eaton Railway Simplex diesel of 1938, fitted with the snowplough supplied to the Eaton Railway in 1897. *J. B. Snell*

Above left:
Green Goddess running into Hythe in August 1964, hauling the *Clayton Pullman* set. These coaches when built were certainly the best and most comfortable 15in gauge stock ever, and even towards the end of their days, minus steam heat and electric light, plus their original upholstery, and with their roofs lowered, they made up a handsome train of strongly LNER appearance. *P. H. Groom*

Centre left:
When new in 1980, the Ravenglass & Eskdale's latest diesel *Lady Wakefield* ran trials for some days on the RH&DR, although clearance problems prevented it running on the Dungeness line. Approaching the Warren with a train for Hythe. *P. H. Groom*

Bottom left:
Typhoon on a train about to leave New Romney for Hythe. *P. H. Groom*

Top:
Night running, particularly with steam power, is now fairly uncommon; when it occurs, the locomotive is fitted with a temporary electric headlight, visible in this shot of *Black Prince* on New Cut Bridge in November 1983. *P. H. Groom*

Right:
Typhoon leaving New Romney for Dungeness. *P. H. Groom*

Events and People

Above:
The railway had its second royal visit in March 1957, when the Queen travelled from New Romney to Hythe. Here she is inspecting *Hurricane* on arrival at Hythe; behind her is Captain Howey speaking to Lord Brabourne, while Prince Philip talks to Prince Charles, who has just been travelling on the locomotive with driver George Barlow. *J. C. Adams*

Above right:
Laurel and Hardy visited the railway in 1947, and more or less formally reopened the Dungeness line after its postwar repairs. Here they prove that they can both fit on the footplate of *Doctor Syn*.

Right:
Tommy Handley and the crew of the radio show 'ITMA' came down in 1948 and also attracted an immense crowd. He stands in the cab of *Green Goddess* with driver Barlow behind; Jack Train and Hattie Jacques on the right.

Top left:
Walt Disney was also a railway enthusiast, and had a miniature line in his own home – and also saw to it that steam trains were prominent in both Disneylands. During his visit to the RH&DR in 1952 he rode on *Green Goddess* with George Barlow.

Top right:
The Hythe to New Romney section was reopened after the war, in spring 1946, by the mayors of the two towns, shaking hands in front of *Hurricane* at Hythe. *Topical*

Above left:
Howey did not much enjoy being photographed and there are few good photographs of him. This one was taken in 1957, at the request of the American author 'Cap' Shaw for his book *Little Railways of the World*. *G. A. Barlow*

Above right:
Following Howey's death in September 1963, the railway was purchased by two retired bankers, S. H. Collins and J. E. Scatcherd. Mr Scatcherd was a sleeping partner, but Mr Collins moved into Howey's house *Red Tiles*, next to the engine shed at New Romney, and kept in close touch with the business. This photograph was taken in the station office (note the wallpaper); on Collins' right is the railway's Manager, Peter Catt, who died suddenly in 1968.

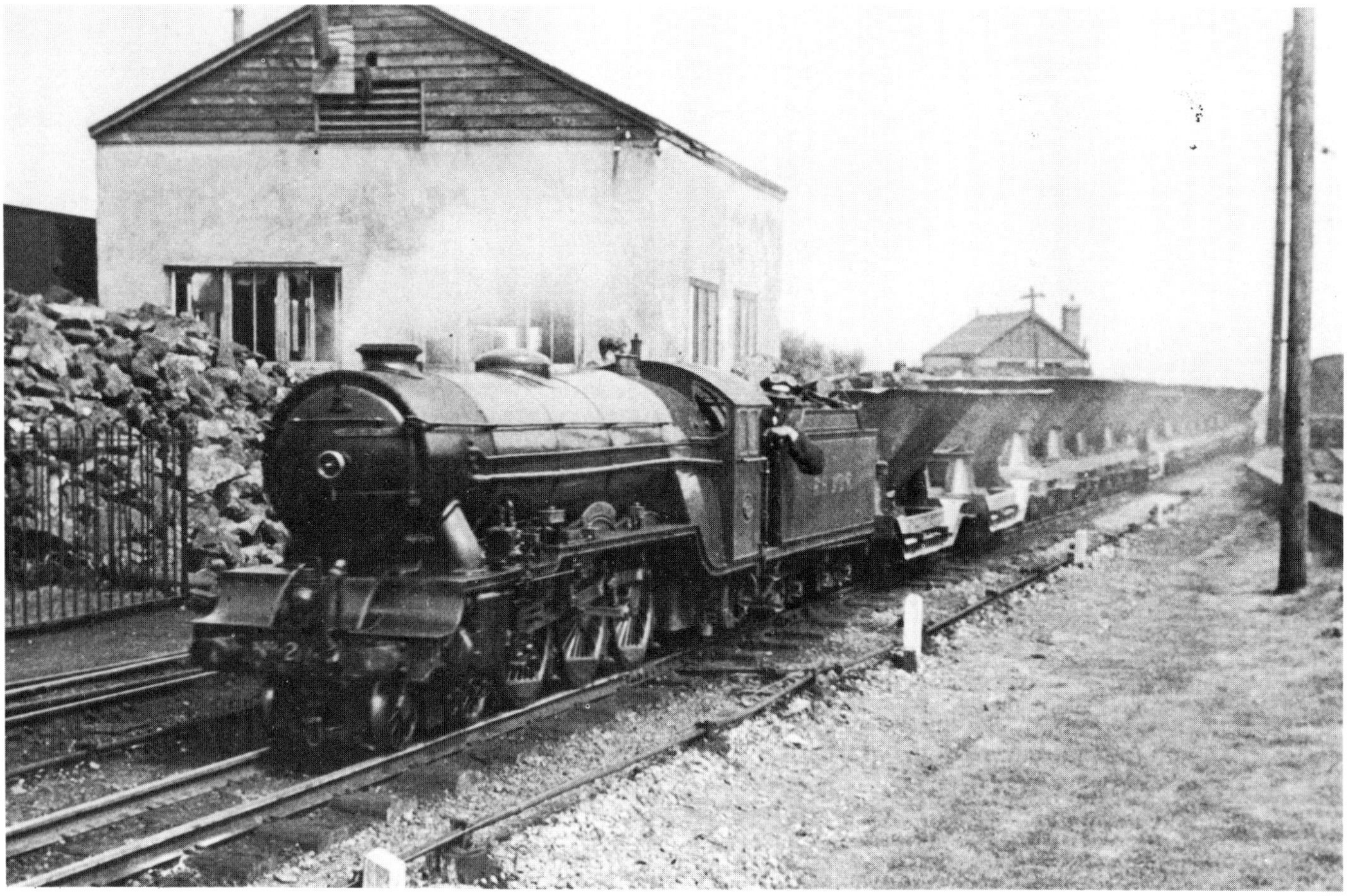

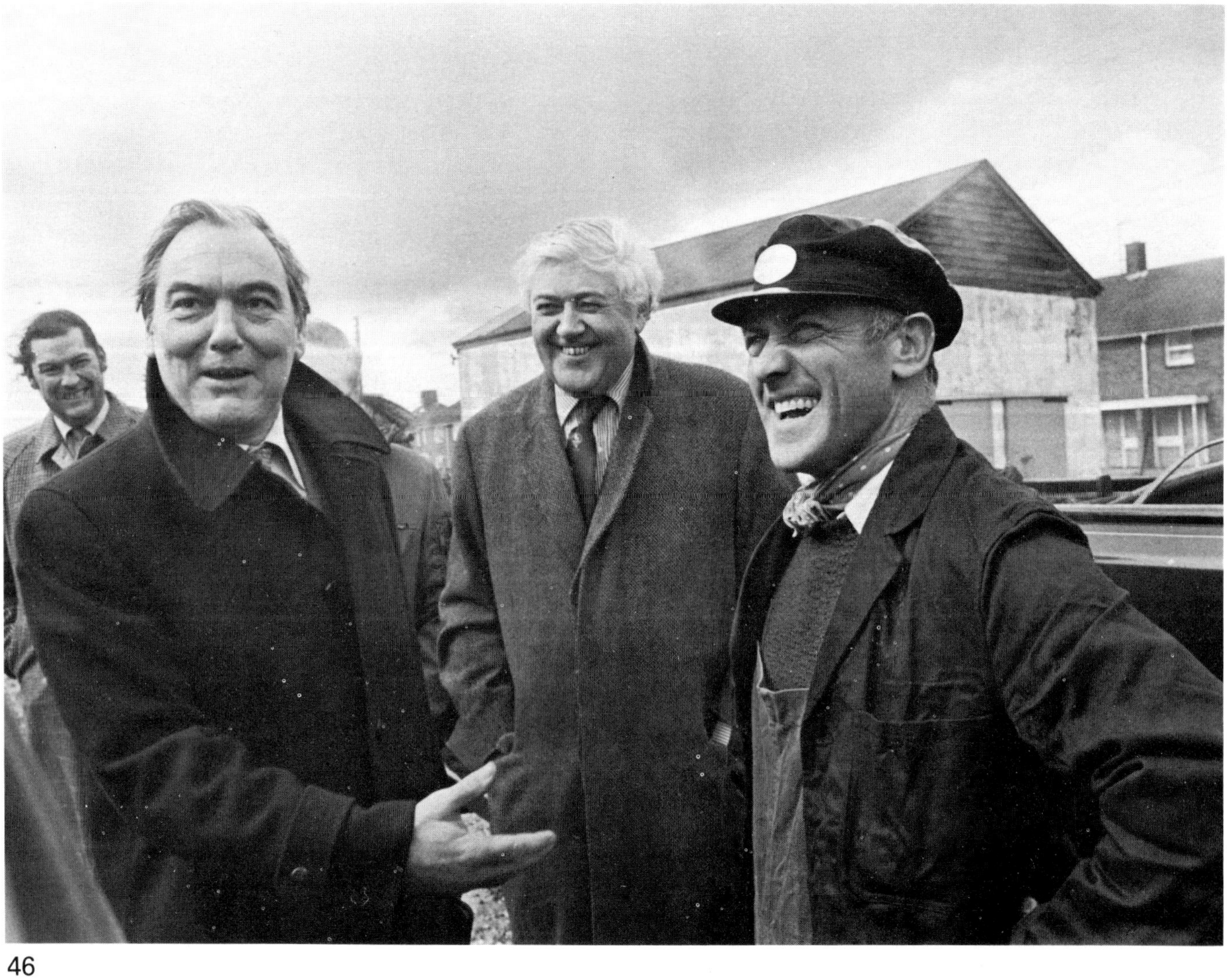

Above left:
Northern Chief on an empty ballast train passing through New Romney station in July 1947. Most of the 60 four-wheeled, one-ton capacity, tipper trucks purchased for this traffic after 1945 were standard 2ft gauge vehicles, remounted on old 15in gauge wagon frames, which produced a truck with a very high centre of gravity when loaded. In an attempt to improve matters, some were mounted on new 15in gauge four-wheeled well frames, including the first two wagons behind the locomotive in this picture. *J. C. Flemons*

Left:
Peter Parker, then Chairman of British Railways, visited the RH&DR in 1978, and is pictured with Lord Garnock, the RH&DR Chairman (centre) and driver Eric Copping. *Folkestone Herald*

Above:
Engine No 9, originally named *Doctor Syn*, was rechristened *Winston Churchill* in 1948 by the great man's grandson, Julian Duncan Sandys, and who was still at school. Standing next to him is the railway's then Manager, Terence Holder.

Right:
George Barlow completed 25 years' service with the railway, and as a regular driver of *Green Goddess* in 1972, and on this anniversary was presented by the railway's then Chairman, Bill McAlpine, not only with a new camera but also with an aluminised firing shovel and cleaning bucket to use on his engine.
A. R. W. Crowhurst

Above:
Doctor Syn pushing some ballast trucks up the ramp to the unloading hoppers at Hythe station; July 1947. The two CPR engines, with sanding gear and better weather protection for the drivers, came into their own on this traffic, particularly in winter. *J. C. Flemons*

Right:
Freight movements on the RH&DR are now quite rare, but during the mid-1970s included delivery of a hundred tons or so of steel pipe to a sewer construction scheme near Dymchurch. Some pipes being loaded onto flat trucks at New Romney. *P. C. Hawkins*

Below:
Looking out of the window of a train arriving at Hythe in 1947, clearly showing the ramped siding to the ballast hoppers, all trace of which has now gone. *H. C. Casserley*